Father Fox's Pe

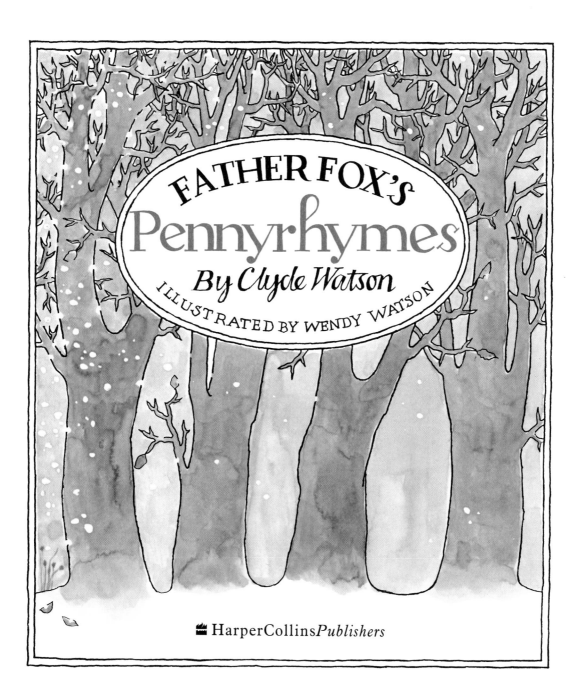

FATHER FOX'S
Pennyrhymes

By Clyde Watson

ILLUSTRATED BY WENDY WATSON

HarperCollins*Publishers*

Father Fox's Pennyrhymes
Reissued in hardcover by HarperCollins*Publishers* in 2001.
Published by arrangement with the author and the illustrator.
Text copyright © 1971 by Clyde Watson
Illustrations copyright © 1971 by Wendy Watson
Printed in the United States of America.
First published in 1971 by the Thomas Y. Crowell Company.
First Harper Trophy edition, 1987.
www.harperchildrens.com

Library of Congress Cataloging-in-Publication Data
Watson, Clyde.
    Father Fox's pennyrhymes/by Clyde Watson ; illustrated by Wendy
Watson.
        p.   cm.
    Summary: Thirty rhymes record the various activities of Father Fox,
his family, and friends.
    ISBN 0-06-029501-5—ISBN 0-06-029502-3 (lib. bdg.)
    1. Nursery rhymes.   2. Children's poetry, American.   [1. Nursery
rhymes.   2. American poetry.]   I. Watson, Wendy, ill.   II. Title.

PZ8.3.W28 Fat   2001
811'.54—dc21   00-047268
                                                                     CIP
                                                                      AC

                        1   2   3   4   5   6   7   8   9   10

FOR NANNY, BECAUSE SHE'S NEAT
FOR CAMMIE, BECAUSE SHE'S SWEET
AND
FOR SOUPSPOON, BECAUSE SHE'S BOTH

The sky is dark, there blows a storm
Our cider is hot, the fire is warm
The snow is deep & the night is long:
Old Father Fox, will you sing us a song?

I

Mister Lister sassed his sister
Married his wife 'cause he couldn't resist her,
Three plus four times two he kissed her:
How many times is that, dear sister?

3

Knickerbocker Knockabout
Sausages & Sauerkraut
Run! Run! Run! The hogs are out!
Knickerbocker Knockabout.

Somersault & Pepper-upper
Simmer down & eat your supper,

Artichokes & Mustard Pickle
Two for a dime or six for a nickel.

Apples for the little ones
And sweets for Christmas morn,
A dear blue bonnet for my wife
And I love barley corn.

Dilly Dilly Piccalilli
Tell me something very silly:
There was a chap his name was Bert
He ate the buttons off his shirt.

II

Country Bumpkin
Pick a pumpkin
Put it in your cart:
For little Jenny
Half-a-penny
Valentine sweetheart.

The rain falls down
The wind blows up:
I've spent all the pennies
In my old tin cup.

See Saw
Jump-in-the-straw
Give me a bone for my
Good dog to gnaw.

See Saw
Jump-in-the-straw
If I were a donkey
I'd cry "Hee-Haw!"

Nanny Banny Bumblebee
Nanny is my cup of tea
I'm as happy as can be
When I've got Nanny on my knee.

20

Knock! Knock! Anybody there?
I've feathers for your caps
And ribbons for your hair.
If you can't pay you can sing me a song,
But if you can't sing, I'll just run along.

Uptown, downtown,
Wrong side to,
Goodness me
What a hullabaloo!

Upstairs, downstairs,
Roundabout,
Backwards, forwards,
Inside OUT!

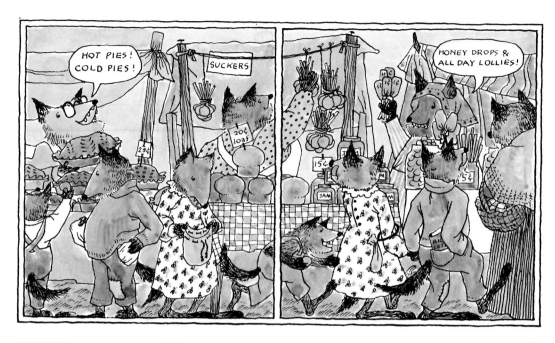

Huckleberry, gooseberry, raspberry pie
All sweetest things one cannot buy.
Peppermint candies are six for a penny,
But true love & kisses, one cannot buy any.

I knew a man
His name was Naught:
I stole his chickens
And I never was caught.

Oh my goodness, oh my dear,
Sassafras & ginger beer,
Chocolate cake & apple punch:
I'm too full to eat my lunch.

Rock, rock, sleep, my baby
Sings the sweet cuckoo . . .
When your Daddy comes back home
He'll bring a toy for you.

Hush, hush, sleep, my baby
Sleep the whole night through . . .
When your Daddy comes back home
He'll sing a song for you.

Miss Quiss!
Look at this!
A pocketful of
Licorice!
You may have some
If you wish,
But every stick will
Cost a kiss.

Penny candy
Sugar hearts
Oranges &
Lemon tarts,

Ask me where my
Money goes?
To buy my sweetheart
Fancy clothes.

33

Happy Birthday, Silly Goose!
Just today we'll let you loose
But if tomorrow you are hooked,
Then my dear, your goose is cooked.

Thomas Thomas Tinkertoes
Upside down & away he goes!
He's off to call upon the Queen
In blue & crimson velveteen.

How many miles to Old Norfolk
To see a magician breathe fire & smoke?
    One, two, three, four,
    Only three miles more.
How many miles to Christmas Cove
To eat of an applecake baked with clove?
    One, two, three, four,
    Only two miles more.

How many miles to Newburyport
For trinkets & sweets of every sort?
    One, two, three, four,
      Only one mile more.
How many miles to Lavender Spring
To hear a fine trumpeter play for the King?
    One, two, three, four,
      Here we are, we'll go no more.

Here's a song of Tinker & Peter
Honey is sweet but love is sweeter . . .
What comes next? Now tell me dearly,
Alexander darling.

Belly & Tubs went out in a boat,
Tubs wore knickers & Belly a coat,
They got in a quarrel & started to shout
And the boat tipped over & they tumbled out.

43

44

Ding, Dong,
Sing me a song,
That way the
Work day is
Not so long.

Little Martha piggy-wig
Run away and dance a jig!
If you weren't so fat and sweet
You wouldn't be so good to eat.

47

There were five fellows
Went to a fair,
They gave their wives no warning:
They jigged & they whistled
And they laughed & they fiddled
'Till early Monday morning.

Pinky Pauper picked my pocket,
Took my darling's silver locket,
I caught him sleeping—eight, nine, ten—
And stole the locket back again.

Ride your red horse down Vinegar Lane,
Gallop, oh gallop, oh gallop again!
Thistles & foxholes & fences beware:
I've seventeen children but none I can spare.

Let the fall leaves fall
And the cold snow snow
And the rain rain rain 'till April:
Our coats are warm
And the pantry's full
And there's cake upon the table.

Soft falls the snow
The coals burn low
Little Jacob's asleep on my knee;
My story ends here
For midnight is near:
To bed now, one-two-three!